"readerpreneurship

A BOOK ABOUT BOOKS

MASTER EDITION

555 QUOTES ON READING FROM THE BEST MINDS OF HUMANITY

Shiromani **Kant**

Dedicated to
All bibliophiles around the world.

INTRODUCTION

I created this book because I myself needed this one.

I discovered the power of reading in 2018 by reading a personal finance bestseller by Robert Kiyosaki - Rich Dad Poor Dad. What an incredibly written book it was. It made me realize how little I know about money and creating wealth. That book was eye-opening. Since then, I haven't stopped reading.

Now, I get excited whenever I read a famous quote from a famous personality appreciating the love for books, It resonates with me a lot.

However, reading is time-consuming and sometimes feels a bit overwhelming as well (at least to me.) So I looked for a book where I can find all the inspirational quotes from famous people I can look up to feel motivated whenever I want to. Unfortunately, I couldn't find one. So.. now you are holding the product of my further actions in your hand.

Through this book, I'm sharing 555 quotes a.k.a words-of-wisdom from many famous philosophers, experts, celebs, writers, and other influential personalities expressing their love for reading to inspire you to read more and more books. ***Consider each quote as the reason why quitting reading shouldn't ever be an option for you.***

I hope you enjoy this book.

Now, flip the page and let's start.

— Shiromani Kant.

If you love non-fiction books...

would be a great pleasure to have you on
my social media community

instagram.com/readerpreneur
twitter.com/readerpreneur

"A reader lives a thousand lives before he dies. The man who never reads lives only one."

— George R.R. Martin

"Read what you love until you love to read."

— **Naval RaviKant**

"'Classic' - a book which people praise and don't read."

— Mark Twain

#3

"Sometimes, you read a book and it fills you with this weird evangelical zeal, and you become convinced that the shattered world will never be put back together unless and until all living humans read the book."

— **John Green**

"The more that you read,

the more things you will know. **The more that you learn,** *the more places you'll go."*

— **Dr. Seuss**

"I find television very educating. Every time somebody turns on the set, I go into the other room and read a book."

— **Groucho Marx**

"The books that the world calls immoral are books that show the world its own shame."

— Oscar Wilde

"Books are a uniquely portable magic."

— Stephen King

"Only the very weak-minde d refuse to be influenced by literature and poetry."

— Cassandra Clare

"Books are the ultimate dumpees: put them down and they'll wait for you forever; pay attention to them and they always love you back."

— John Green

#**10**

"Books are the quietest and most constant of friends; they are the most accessible and wisest of counselors, and the most patient of teachers."

— **Charles W. Eliot**

"You don't have to burn books to destroy a culture. Just get people to stop reading them."

— Ray Bradbury

"Let us read, and let us dance; these two amusements will never do any harm to the world."

— **Voltaire**

#**13**

"Formal education will make you a living; self-education will make you a fortune."

— Jim Rohn

"Successful people have libraries. The rest have big-screen TVs."

— Jim Rohn

"Read 500 pages...
every day. That's how
knowledge works. *It
builds up, like
compound interest.* All
of you can do it, but I
guarantee not many
of you will do it."

— Warren Buffett

"Each book you read not only teaches you something new, but also opens up different ways of thinking about old ideas. As Warren Buffet says 'That's how knowledge works. It builds up, like compound interest'."

— James Clear

"Reading is the ultimate meta-skill that can be traded for anything else."

— Naval RaviKant

"There is more treasure in books than in all the pirate's loot on Treasure Island."

— **Walt Disney**

"I love books, by the way, way more than movies. Movies tell you what to think. A good book lets you choose a few thoughts for yourself."

— **Karen Marie Moning**

"Skim a lot of books. Read a few. *Immediately re-read the best ones twice.*"

— Shane Parrish

"Reading is still the main way that I both learn new things and test my understanding."

— Bill Gates

"Reading maketh a full man; conference a ready man; and writing an exact man."

— Sir Francis Bacon

"Before you move on to the normal bustle of the day, invest in yourself. **Before your life turns into a whirlwind of activity, read a book that will make you better.**"

— James Clear

"Libraries raised me."

— **Ray Bradbury**

"We become the books we read."

— **Matthew Kelly**

#26

"The difference between where you are today and where you'll be five years from now will be found in the quality of books you've read."

— **Jim Rohn**

#**27**

"In my whole life, I have known no wise people (over a broad subject matter area) who didn't read all the time – none, zero."

— Charlie Munger

"You get a little moody sometimes but I think that's because you like to read. People that like to read are always a little fucked up."

— **Pat Conroy**

#29

"In the case of good books, the point is not to see how many of them you can get through, but rather *how many can get through to you.*"

— Mortimer J. Adler

"Read, read, read. Read everything – trash, classics, good and bad, and see how they do it. Just like a carpenter who works as an apprentice and studies the master. Read! You'll absorb it. Then write. If it's good, you'll find out. If it's not, throw it out of the window."

— **William Faulkner**

"*Think before you speak.* **Read before you think.**"

— Fran Lebowitz

"Books are mirrors: you only see in them what you already have inside you."

— **Carlos Ruiz Zafón**

"Reader's Bill of Rights:
1. The right to not read
2. The right to skip pages
3. The right to not finish
4. The right to reread
5. The right to read anything
6. The right to escapism
7. The right to read anywhere
8. The right to browse
9. The right to read out loud
10. The right to not defend your tastes"

— **Daniel Pennac**

"There are worse crimes than burning books. One of them is not reading them."

— Joseph Brodsky

"We live for books."

— **Umberto Eco**

#36

"I cannot remember the books I've read any more than the meals I have eaten; even so, *they have made me*."

— Ralph Waldo Emerson

"A good book is an event in my life."

— Stendhal

"Once you have read a book you care about, some part of it is always with you."

— **Louis L'Amour**

#39

"The advice I would give is to read everything in sight. And to start very young. It's a huge advantage in almost any field to start young. If that's where your interest lies, and you start young, and you read a lot, you're going to you're going to do well."

— Warren Buffett

"Everything in the world exists in order to end up as a book."

— Stéphane Mallarmé

#**41**

"A peasant that reads is a prince in waiting."

— **Walter Mosley**

"Books are the plane, and the train, and the road. They are the destination and the journey. They are home."

— Anna Quindlen

"I can survive well enough on my own — if given the proper reading material."

— **Sarah J. Maas**

"The best moments in reading are when you come across something – a thought, a feeling, a way of looking at things – which you had thought special and particular to you. Now here it is, set down by someone else, a person you have never met, someone even who is long dead. And it is as if a hand has come out and taken yours."

— **Alan Bennett**

#**45**

"Books to the ceiling,
Books to the sky,
My pile of books is a
mile high.
How I love them!
How I need them!
I'll have a long
beard by the time I
read them."

— **Arnold Lobel**

"Many people, myself among them, feel better at the mere sight of a book."

— Jane Smiley

"I owe everything I am and everything I will ever be to books."

— **Gary Paulsen**

#48

"Books break the shackles of time — proof that humans can work magic."

— **Carl Sagan**

"If you don't like to read, you haven't found the right book."

— J.K Rowling

"Read the best books first, or you may not have a chance to read them at all."

— **Henry David Thoreau**

"Books are finite, sexual encounters are finite, but the desire to read and to fuck is infinite; it surpasses our own deaths, our fears, our hopes for peace."

— **Roberto Bolano**

"No matter how busy you may think you are, you must find time for reading, or surrender yourself to self-chosen ignorance."

— **Atwood H. Townsend**

#**53**

"What a man reads pours massive ingredients into his mental factory and the fabric of his life is built from those ingredients."

— Jim Rohn

"It is better to know one book intimately than a hundred superficially."

— Donna Tartt

#**55**

"Once you learn to read, you will be forever free."

— **Frederick Douglass**

"What a blessing it is to love books."

— **Elizabeth von Arnim**

"Reading can teach you the best of what others already know. Reflection can teach you the best of what only you can know."

— James Clear

"Everybody can read what I read, it is a level playing field."

— **Warren Buffett**

#**59**

"A classic is a book that has never finished saying what it has to say."

— **Italo Calvino**

"Reading furnishes the mind only with materials of knowledge; it is thinking that makes what we read ours."

— John Locke

"Reading is the sole means by which we slip, involuntarily, often helplessly, into another's skin, another's voice, another's soul."

— Joyce Carol Oates

"For some of us, books are as important as almost anything else on earth. What a miracle it is that out of these small, flat, rigid squares of paper unfolds world after world after world, worlds that sing to you, comfort and quiet or excite you. Books help us understand who we are and how we are to behave. They show us what community and friendship mean; they show us how to live and die."

— **Anne Lamott**

"Properly, we should read for power. Man reading should be man intensely alive. The book should be a ball of light in one's hand."

— **Ezra Pound**

"The greatest gift is the passion for reading.
It is cheap, it consoles, it distracts, it excites,
it gives you knowledge of the world and experience of a wide kind. It is a moral illumination."

— **Elizabeth Hardwick**

"Spend your time in the company of geniuses, sages, children, and books."

— Naval RaviKant

"Reading, after a certain age, diverts the mind too much from its creative pursuits. Any man who reads too much and uses his own brain too little falls into lazy habits of thinking."

— **Albert Einstein**

"The world belongs to those who read."

— Rick Holland

"You will find
most books
worth reading
are worth
reading twice."

— **John Morley**

#69

"Books are the quietest and most constant of friends; they are the most accessible and wisest of counselors, and the most patient of teachers."

— **Charles William Elliot**

"A Book is a gift you can open again and again."

— **Garrison Keillor**

#71

"Develop into a lifelong self-learner through voracious reading; cultivate curiosity and strive to become a little wiser every day."

— Charlie Munger

"Books allow you to fully explore a topic and immerse yourself in a deeper way than most media today."

— **Mark Zuckerberg**

#**73**

"I read books."

— **Elon Musk** (when asked how he learned to build rockets)

"I can feel infinitely alive curled up on the sofa reading a book."

— **Benedict Cumberbatch**

#**75**

"Read. Read. Read. Just don't read one type of book. Read different books by various authors so that you develop different style."

— R.L. Stine

#76

"A library is a place where you can lose your innocence without losing your virginity."

— **Germaine Greer**

#**77**

"A word after a word after a word is power."

— **Margaret Atwood**

"Take a good book to bed with you — books do not snore."

— **Thea Dorn**

#79

"As long as I have a book in my hand, I don't feel like I'm wasting time."

— Charlie Munger

#80

"It isn't what
the book costs.
*It's what it will
cost you if you
don't read it.*"

— Jim Rohn

"Reading brings us unknown friends"

— **Honore de Balzac**

"Rainy days should be spent at home with a cup of tea and a good book."

— **Bill Watterson**

"All I have learned, I learned from books."

— Abraham Lincoln

"You will learn most things by looking, but reading gives understanding. Reading will make you free."

— Paul Rand

"I think its helps to read broadly, what good does it do to know everything about one little thing if you don't know how it fits into the world, and how the world is going to effect it."

— Howard Marks

#86

"I read for pleasure and that is the moment I learn the most."

— **Margaret Atwood**

#**87**

"There are many little ways to enlarge your world. Love of books is the best of all."

— Jacqueline Kennedy

#88

"What I love most about reading: It gives you the ability to reach higher ground. And keep climbing."

— **Oprah Winfrey**

#89

"In principle
and reality,
libraries are
life-enhancing
palaces of
wonder."

— **Gail Honeyman**

"He that loves reading has everything within his reach."

— William Godwin

"Books can be dangerous. The best ones should be labeled *'This could change your life.'*"

— **Helen Exley**

#92

"Reading without reflecting is like eating without digesting."

— Edmund Burke

"No entertainment is so cheap as reading, nor any pleasure so lasting."

— **Mary Wortley Montagu**

"If you would tell me the heart of a man, tell me not what he reads, but what he rereads."

— François Mauriac

"The reading of all good books is like a conversation with the finest men of past centuries."

— René Descartes

"The problem with a life spent reading is you know too much."

— Josh Lanyon

"Read. As much as you can. As deeply and widely and nourishingly and irritatingly as you can. And the good things will make you remember them, so you won't need to take notes."

— A.L. Kennedy

"Not all readers
are leaders,
but all leaders
are readers."

— **Harry Truman**

#**99**

"Reading has given me more perspective on a number of topics -- from science to religion, from poverty to prosperity, from health to energy to social justice, from political philosophy to foreign policy, and from history to futuristic fiction. This challenge has been intellectually fulfilling, and I come away with a greater sense of hope and optimism that our society can make greater progress in all of these areas."

— **Mark Zuckerberg**

"Books are
no more
threatened
by Kindle
than stairs by
elevators."

— Stephen Fry

"The oldest
books are still
only just out
to those who
have not read
them."

— **Samuel Butler**

"Most of what makes a book 'good' is that we are reading it at the right moment for us."

— Alain de Botton

#103

"Sit in a room and read - and read and read. And read the right books by the right people. Your mind is brought onto that level, and you have a nice, mild, slow-burning rapture all the time."

— **Joseph Campbell**

#104

"Keep reading. It's one of the most marvelous adventures that anyone can have."

— Lloyd Alexander

"Reading is
to the mind
what exercise
is to the body."

— Joseph Addison

"Read more books than those who have a formal education, developing this into a lifelong habit."

— **Robert Greene**

#**107**

"Miss a meal if you have to, but don't miss a book."

— Jim Rohn

"A book is not completed till it's read."

— **Salman Rushdie**

"You should never read just for "enjoyment." Read to make yourself smarter! Less judgmental. More apt to understand your friends' insane behavior, or better yet, your own."

— **John Waters**

"When writers die they become books, which is, after all, not too bad an incarnation."

— Jorge Luis Borges

"The problem with books is that they end."

— **Caroline Kepnes**

"When we read, another person thinks for us: we merely repeat his mental process."

— **Arthur Schopenhauer**

#**113**

"I just sit in my office and read all day."

— **Warren Buffett**

"If all printers were determined not to print anything till they were sure it would offend nobody, there would be very little printed."

— **Benjamin Franklin**

"If you truly love a book, you should sleep with it, write in it, read aloud from it, and fill its pages with muffin crumbs."

— Anne Fadiman

"Books are not made for furniture, but there is nothing else that so beautifully furnishes a house."

— Henry Ward Beecher

"Let's be reasonable and add an eighth day to the week that is devoted exclusively to reading."

— Lena Dunham

"The ability to read awoke inside of me some long dormant craving to be mentally alive."

— Malcolm X

"Reading is important. If you know how to read, then the whole world opens up to you."

— **Barack Obama**

"My best friend is a person who will give me a book I have not read."

— **Abraham Lincoln**

"Almost everything I have read has been useful to me — science, poetry, politics, novels. I have a lifelong interest in epistemology and learning. My books have helped me develop a way of thinking critically in business."

— **Sidney Harman**

"The only thing worse than not reading a book in the last ninety days is not reading a book in the last ninety days and thinking that it doesn't matter."

— Jim Rohn

#123

"I would continuously search for new ideas. I read every book and magazine I could. Heck, 3 bucks for a magazine, 20 bucks for a book. One good idea that led to a customer or solution and it paid for itself many times over."

— **Mark Cuban**

"If you get into the mental habit of relating what you're reading to the basic structure of the underlying ideas being demonstrated, you gradually accumulate some wisdom."

— Charlie Munger

#125

"Reading is essential for those who seek to rise above the ordinary."

— Jim Rohn

"Reading well is one of the great pleasures that solitude can afford you."

— Harold Bloom

"You see, unlike in the movies, there is no THE END sign flashing at the end of books. When I've read a book, I don't feel like I've finished anything. So I start a new one."

— **Elif Shafak**

#128

"What we become depends on what we read after all of the professors have finished with us. The greatest university of all is a collection of books."

— **Thomas Carlyle**

"Reading's the only thing that allows you to use your imagination. When you watch films it's someone else's vision, isn't it?"

— Lemmy Kilmister

"You want to remember that while you're judging the book, the book is also judging you."

— Stephen King

"A writer only begins a book. A reader finishes it."

— Samuel Johnson

"When I am king they shall not have bread and shelter only, but also teachings out of books, for a full belly is little worth where the mind is starved."

— **Mark Twain**

"When you pick up a good book you feel it instantly. Not only are they well written and packed with ideas and insight, but they're well organized. You want to read the next page."

— Shane Parrish

"The things that change your life are: the people you meet, the classes you take, and the books you read."

— **Jim Rohn**

"Reading is a basic tool in the living of a good life."

— **Mortimer J. Adler**

"We read a lot. I don't know anyone who's wise who doesn't read a lot. But that's not enough: You have to have a temperament to grab ideas and do sensible things. Most people don't grab the right ideas or don't know what to do with them."

— **Charlie Munger**

"There are plenty of excellent articles on the web, but generally speaking, the quality of good books is better. Books typically have better writing (more tightly edited) and higher quality information (better fact-checking and more extensive research). From a learning perspective, it's probably a better use of my time to read books than to read online content."

— **James Clear**

#138

"If you read everyday, you will eventually develop expertise."

— Greg McKeown

"Everything I read was public. Anyone could buy the same books and magazines. The same information was available to anyone who wanted it. Turns out most people didn't want it. Most people won't put in the time to get a knowledge advantage."

— **Mark Cuban**

"Books that don't deliver timeless insights don't stick around. Time filters out what works from what doesn't. And there is no need to waste time on ones that don't last."

— Shane Parrish

"The book you don't read can't help."

— Jim Rohn

"I don't think you can get to be a really good investor over a broad range without doing a massive amount of reading. I don't think any one book will do it for you."

— **Charlie Munger**

#143

"Reading consumes time. And if we equate time with money, it should not be wasted on bad books."

— Shane Parrish

"One can never read too little of bad, or too much of good books: bad books are intellectual poison; they destroy the mind."

— Arthur Schopenhauer

#145

"If you only read the books that everyone else is reading, you can only think what everyone else is thinking."

— Haruki Murakami

"Marking a book is literally an experience of your differences or agreements with the author. It is the highest respect you can pay him."

— Edgar Allen Poe

"Learning something insightful requires mental work. It's uncomfortable. **If it doesn't hurt, you're not learning.** You need to find writers who are more knowledgeable on a particular subject than yourself. By narrowing the gap between the author and yourself, you get smarter."

— **Shane Parrish**

"With my eyes closed, I would touch a familiar book and draw its fragrance deep inside me. This was enough to make me happy."

— Haruki Murakami

#149

"Everything you need for a better future and success has already been written. And guess what? All you have to do is go to the library."

— Jim Rohn

"I really had a lot of dreams when I was a kid, and I think a great deal of that grew out of the fact that I had a chance to read a lot."

— **Bill Gates**

#151

"I have never known any distress that an hour's reading did not relieve."

— **Montesquieu**

#152

"If one reads enough books one has a fighting chance. Or better, one's chances of survival increase with each book one reads."

— Sherman Alexie

#153

"We should read to give our souls a chance to luxuriate."

— **Henry Miller**

"One of the benefits of reading is that it allows you to master the best of what other people have already figured out. This is only true, however, if you can remember and apply the lessons and insights from what you read."

— **Shane Parrish**

#155

"There is no such thing as a child who hates to read; there are only children who have not found the right book."

— **Frank Serafini**

"Books and doors are the same thing. You open them, and you go through into another world."

— Jeanette Winterson

"You'd be amazed at how much Warren reads – at how much I read. My children laugh at me. They think I'm a book with a couple of legs sticking out."

— **Charlie Munger**

#158

"I think books are like people, in the sense that they'll turn up in your life when you most need them."

— Emma Thompson

#159

"Read a book
because you
are passionate
about the
subject."

— Jay Shetty

"The trick is to teach yourself to read in small sips as well as long swallows."

— Stephen King

"Read. Read anything. Read the things they say are good for you, and the things they claim are junk. You'll find what you need to find. Just read."

— **Neil Gaiman**

"Be curious.
Read widely.
Try new things.
What people
call intelligence
just boils down
to curiosity."

— Aaron Swartz

#163

"Buying books would be a good thing if one could also buy the time to read them; but as a rule the purchase of books is mistaken for the appropriation of their contents."

— **Arthur Schopenhauer**

"All that mankind has done, thought, gained, or been; it is lying as in magic preservation in the pages of books."

— **Thomas Carlyle**

#165

"I read the fuck out of every book I can get my hands on."

— **Nick Hornby**

"Just handle
the books
gently and
you'll get
along fine."

— Patrick Rothfuss

"I knew right there in prison that reading had forever changed the course of my life."

— Malcolm X

"Literature is the art of discovering something extraordinary about ordinary people, and saying with ordinary words something extraordinary."

— **Boris Pasternak**

#169

"I like books that aren't just lovely but that have memories in themselves. Just like playing a song, picking up a book again that has memories can take you back to another place or another time."

— Emma Watson

"The keys to life
are running
and reading."

- Will Smith

"Don't read a book and be a follower; read a book and be a student."

— Jim Rohn

#172

"As we expand our knowledge of good books, we shrink the circle of men whose company we appreciate."

— Ludwig Feuerbach

#173

"The buying of more books than one can read is nothing less than the soul reaching toward infinity."

— A. Edward Newton

#174

"Reading is thinking with someone else's head instead of one's own."

— Arthur Schopenhauer

#175

"Reading time is limited, it should be directed at the knowledge that lasts. The opportunity cost of reading something new is re-reading the best book you've ever read."

— **Shane Parrish**

"Come to the book as you would come to an unexplored land. Come without a map. Explore it and draw your own map."

— Stephen King

"I have never been able to resist a book about books."

— Anne Fadiman

"Get books, sit yourself down anywhere, and go to reading them yourself."

— Abraham Lincoln

#179

"Entering a novel is like going on a climb in the mountains: you have to learn the rhythm of respiration, acquire the pace; otherwise you stop right away."

— **Umberto Eco**

#180

"Buying a book is not about obtaining a possession, but about securing a portal."

— Laura Miller

#181

"I read a lot. I love books. If they came in a bottle, I'd be a drunk too."

— Alyxandra Harvey

#**182**

"Think of this - that the writer wrote alone, and the reader read alone, and they were alone with each other."

— A.S. Byatt

#183

"You almost have to read the stuff you're reading, because you're into it. You don't need any other reason. There's no mission here to accomplish. Just read because you enjoy it."

— Naval RaviKant

#184

"I've not found! one single mutual fund, one single real estate investment, any gold, silver or anything else that has given me higher returns than: me investing in myself."

— **Patrick Bet-David**

"Reading a book is among the most high-leverage activities on earth."

— Greg McKeown

"The man who does not read has no advantage over the man who cannot read."

— Mark Twain

#187

"I have always imagined paradise will be kind of library."

— Jorge Luis Borges

#188

"Beware you be not swallowed up in books! An ounce of love is worth a pound of knowledge."

— John Wesley

"A fool may buy all the books in the world, and they will be in his library; but he will be able to read only those that he deserves to."

— Swami Vivekananda

"It is not true that 'we have only one life to live'; if we can read, we can live as many more lives and as many kinds of lives as we wish."

— S.I. Hayakawa

"Once a book has been read, it never looks the same again."

— Shiromani Kant

"I often feel sorry for people who don't read good books; they are missing a chance to lead an extra life."

— Scott Corbett

#193

"Reading an hour a day is only 4% of your day. But that 4% will put you at the top of your field within 10 years. Find the time."

— Patrick Bet-David

"Any book
worth banning
is a book worth
reading."

— **Isaac Asimov**

"Whether I'm at the office, at home, or on the road, I always have a stack of books I'm looking forward to reading."

— Bill Gates

#196

"Every reader exists to ensure for a certain book a modest immortality. Reading is, in this sense, a ritual of rebirth."

— **Alberto Manguel**

"Never force yourself to read a book that you do not enjoy. There are so many good books in the world that it is foolish to waste time on one that does not give you pleasure."

— **Atwood H. Townsend**

"There are no short cuts to mental fitness. Much like compound interest, reading has compounding benefits."

— Christopher Begg

#199

"In reading we must become creators."

— **Madeleine L'Engle**

"Reading is where the wild things are."

—Jeanette Winterson

"**Read voraciously and wait patiently, and from time to time these amazing bets will present themselves."**

— Mohnish Pabrai

"You can be too rich and too thin, but you can never be too well read or too curious about the world."

— Tim Gunn

"Nothing was truly unbearable if you had something to read."

— Jincy Willett

"Read, read, read, read, read, read, read, read, read, read, read, read, read...if you don't read, you will never be a filmmaker."

— **Werner Herzog** (filmmaker)

#205

"His money went largely toward books, which to him were like sacred objects, providing ballast for his mind."

— **Michelle Obama**, describing about Barack Obama

"Reading a book doesn't mean just turning the pages. It means thinking about it, identifying parts that you want to go back to, asking how to place it in a broader context, pursuing the ideas. There's no point in reading a book if you let it pass before your eyes and then forget about it ten minutes later. Reading a book is an intellectual exercise, which stimulates thought, questions, imagination."

— **Noam Chomsky**

#207

"Read not to contradict and confute, nor to believe and take for granted ...but to weigh and consider."

— Francis Bacon

"When it comes
to reading,
make sure your
foundation is
very, very high
quality."

— Naval RaviKant

"Reading the Bible will help you get to know the word, but it's when you put it down and live your life that you get to know the author."

— Steve Maraboli

"I love bookshelves, and stacks of books, spines, typography, and the feel of pages between my fingertips."

— Laini Taylor

"You will learn most things by looking, but reading gives understanding. Reading will make you free."

— **Paul Rand**

"Books are for people who wish they were somewhere else."

— **Mark Twain**

"Reading — A Gentleman's Habit."

— Shiromani Kant

"Education...has produced a vast population able to read but unable to distinguish what is worth reading."

— George Macaulay Trevelyan

#215

"Young men, especially in America, write to me and ask me to recommend "a course of reading." Distrust a course of reading! People who really care for books read all of them. There is no other course."

— **Andrew Lang**

#216

"If a book isn't self-explanatory, then it isn't worth reading."

— Paulo Coelho

"I read in self-defense."

— **Woody Allen**

"You can never be wise unless you love reading."

— Samuel Johnson

"You see, one of the best things about reading is that you'll always have something to think about when you're not reading."

— James Patterson

#220

"Books are like
truth serum -
if you don't
read, you can't
figure out
what's real."

— Rodman Philbrick

"Read a lot. Expect
something big,
something exalting or
deepening from a
book. No book is worth
reading that isn't
worth re-reading."

— Susan Sontag

#222

"Being rich is not about how many homes you own. It's the freedom to pick up any book you want without looking at the price and wondering whether you can afford it."

— John Waters

#223

"Reading enables me to maintain a sense of something substantive– my ethical integrity, my intellectual integrity."

— **Jonathan Franzen**

"Reading is a gift.
It's something
you can do
almost anytime
and anywhere."

— **Richard Carlson**

"The only thing that you absolutely have to know, is the location of the library."

— **Albert Einstein**

"My father always said, 'Never trust anyone whose TV is bigger than their book shelf' - so I make sure I read."

— Emilia Clarke

#227

"The public library is where place and possibility meet."

— Stuart Dybek

#**228**

"The only advice anybody can give is if you want to be a writer, keep writing. And read all you can, read everything."

— Stan Lee

#229

"Before you sleep, read something that is exquisite, and worth remembering."

— Desiderius Erasmus

"Our private tastes in books showed a hint of our secret selves."

— **Nova Ren Suma**

#**231**

"The ability to read becomes devalued when what one has learned to read adds nothing of importance to one's life."

— Bruno Bettelheim

"When I was in my twenties and broke, I'd buy books before food. A meal will sustain you for a few hours, a good book will sustain you for life."

— **Gabrielle Zevin**

"Reading not only educates, but is relaxing and allows you to feed your imagination – creating beautiful pictures from carefully chosen words."

— Eric Ripert

"There's no better way to inform and expand you mind on a regular basis than to get into the habit of reading good literature."

— Stephen R. Covey

"I must judge for myself, but how can I judge, how can any man judge, unless his mind has been opened and enlarged by reading."

— **John Adams**

"When at last I came upon the right book, the feeling was violent: it blew open a hole in me that made life more dangerous because I couldn't control what came through it."

— **Nicole Krauss**

#237

"Maybe Heaven will be a library and then I might get to finish my 'to-read' list."

— **Kellie Elmore**

#238

"My early and invincible love of reading - I would not exchange for the treasures of India."

— **Edward Gibbon**

#239

"A capacity, and taste, for reading, gives access to whatever has already been discovered by others. It is the key, or one of the keys, to the already solved problems. And not only so. It gives a relish, and facility, for successfully pursuing the [yet] unsolved ones."

— **Abraham Lincoln**

"When you sell a man a book you don't sell him just 12 ounces of paper and ink and glue - you sell him a whole new life."

— Christopher Morley

"Books are both our luxuries and our daily bread."

— **Henry Stevens**

#242

"I learned to write by reading the kind of books I wished I'd written."

— **Barbara Kingsolver**

"There is no proper time and place for reading. When the mood for reading comes, one can read anywhere"

— Lin Yutang

"Can there be any greater pleasure than to come across an author one enjoys and then to find they have written not just one book or two, but at least a dozen?"

— **Alan Bennett**

#245

"A book is the cheapest ticket you will ever hold."

— Stefanos Livos

"We human beings build houses because we're alive but we write books because we're mortal."

— Daniel Pennac

"I'm not saying
that you have to
be a reader to
save your soul in
the modern
world. I'm saying
it helps."

— **Walter Mosely**

#248

"Reading is an addiction that I adore."

— **Vianka Van Bokkem**

"The function of a book is to provide a reading experience."

— Douglas Rushkoff

#250

"Like the bodies of dancers or athletes, the minds of readers are genuinely happy and self-possessed only when cavorting around, doing their stretches and leaps and jumps to the tune of words."

— Lynne Sharon Schwartz

#251

"Most non-readers are nothing but an agglomeration of third-hand opinion and blindly received wisdom."

— Tom Bissell

"Life happened because I turned the pages."

— Alberto Manguel

"Reading to small children is a specialty."

— **Clifton Fadiman**

"Reading had never let me down before. It had always been the one sure thing."

— **Diane Setterfield**

"The man who is fond of books is usually a man of lofty thought, and elevated opinions."

— Christopher Dawson

"Make your own Bible. Select and collect all the words and sentences that in all your readings have been to you like the blast of a trumpet."

— Ralph Waldo Emerson

"Reading is not life. Reading is creating life in your head. And that can only help you so much in a storm."

— **David Levithan**

"Study logic and math, because once you've mastered them, you won't fear any book."

— Naval RaviKant

#259

"Home is where your books are."

— Kerstin Gier

"Books are absent teachers."

— Mortimer Adler

#261

"A book can give you an experience of someone's life in a few hours, and this is far more profitable than any sale that's going on."

— **Neeraj Agnihotri**

#262

"Stories are the wealth of humanity!"

— Pierce Brown

"I am a machine condemned to devour books."

— **Karl Marx**

#264

"I would rather read a mediocre book than waste time sitting around with people making small talk."

— **James D. Sass**

#265

"I can think of no better way to become more intelligent than sit down and read."

— Warren Buffett

#266

"You'll never be alone if you've got a book."

— **Al Pacino**

#267

"Reading alters the appearance of a book. Once it has been read, it never looks the same again, and people leave their individual imprint on a book they have read."

— Paul Theroux

#268

"Reading is not simply an intellectual pursuit but an emotional and spiritual one. It lights the candle in the hurricane lamp of self; that's why it survives."

— Anna Quindlen

"When I get hold of a book I particularly admire, I am so enthusiastic that I loan it to someone who never brings it back."

— Edgar Watson Howe

#270

"I'm afraid I've degenerated into a bibliophile."

— Christopher Paolini

"You know that song you can't get out of your head? All thoughts work that way. **Careful what you read."**

— **Naval RaviKant**

#272

"I read, and, in reading, lifted the Curtains of the Impossible that blind the mind, and looked out into the unknown."

— William Hope Hodgson

"A blessed companion is a book - a book that, fitly chosen, is a lifelong friend...a book that, at a touch, pours its heart into your own."

— Douglas Jerrold

#274

"What's cheaper than a gallon of gas? An ebook. Save a dollar, stay home and read!"

— **Shandy L. Kurth**

#275

"Books are the perfect entertainment: no commercials, no batteries,hours of enjoyment for each dollar spent."

— Stephen King

#276

"The power of reading a great book is that you start thinking like the author."

— Tony Robbins

"The reason that reading is so important, there have mean millions and billions and billions and gazillions of people that have lived before all of us, there's no new problem you can have, with your parents, with school, with a bully, with anything. There's no problem you can have that someone hasn't already solved and wrote about it in a book."

— **Will Smith**

#278

"The true reader reads every work seriously in the sense that he reads it whole-heartedly, makes himself as receptive as he can."

— C.S. Lewis

"Statistically, if you're reading this sentence, you're an oddball. The average American spends three minutes a day reading a book. At this moment, you and I are engaged in an essentially antiquated interaction. Welcome, fellow Neanderthal!"

— **Dick Meyer**

#280

"Another thing I need to do, when I'm near the end of the book, is sleep in the same room with it...Somehow the book doesn't leave you when you're asleep right next to it."

— Joan Didion

"A good reading strengthens the soul."

— **Toba Beta**

#**282**

"Reading is sometimes an ingenious device for avoiding thought."

— **Austin Phelps**

#283

"It is a good rule after reading a new book, never to allow yourself another new one till you have read an old one in between."

— C. S. Lewis

"Reading is an activity of civilized beings."

— Toba Beta

"Reality doesn't always give us the life that we desire, but we can always find what we desire between the pages of books."

— Adelise M. Cullens

#286

"Reading was the only amusement I allowed myself."

— Benjamin Franklin

"Who wants a library full of books you've already read?"

— Harlan Ellison

#288

"Literature cannot be imposed; it must be discovered."

— Amy Joy

#289

"You may have tangible wealth untold; caskets of jewels and coffers of gold. Richer than I you can never be. I had a mother who read to me."

— **Strickland Gillian**

#290

"Read voraciously. Learn more broadly about behaviour, philosophy of thinking, biographies and history. Get a sense of the possible. Look at the repeating cycles in human history. There's an abundance of material out there, so you can build your own invisible board of directors, if you will. That's incredibly important."

— Matthew McLennan

"Books are those faithful mirrors that reflect to our mind the minds of sages and heroes."

— **Edward Gibbon**

"I don't need
no Smith and
Wesson, man,
I got Merriam
and Webster."

— Avi Steinberg

"Every new book we read in our brief and busy lives means that a classic is left unread."

— B.R. Myers

"Reading messed with my brain in an unaccountable way. It made me happy; or something."

— Salvatore Scibona

#295

"Life is limited, but by writing, and reading, we can live in different worlds, get inside the skins and minds of other people, and, in this way, push out the boundaries of our own lifes."

— **Joan Lingard**

"The more you read, the better you're going to become as a storyteller."

— Stan Lee

"There are treasures in books that all the money in the world cannot buy, but the poorest laborer can have for nothing."

— **Robert Ingersoll**

#298

"There's a book for everyone, even if they don't think there is. A book that reaches in and grabs your soul."

— Veronica Henry

#299

"Collect books, even if you don't plan on reading them right away. Filmmaker John Waters has said, "Nothing is more important than an unread library."

— Austin Kleon

"The delights of reading impart the vivacity of youth even to old age."

— Isaac D'Israeli

#301

"The best book is not one that informs merely, but one that stirs the reader up to inform himself."

— A.W. Tozer

#302

"There is much you can learn from books and scrolls. These books are my friends, my companions. They make me laugh and cry and find meaning in life."

— Christopher Paolini

#303

"An attentive reader will always learn more, and more quickly, from good authors than from life."

— Hervé Le Tellier

"No amount of reading or memorizing will make you successful in life. It is the understanding and application of wise thought that counts."

— **Bob Proctor**

"Give yourself to reading."

— Charles Spurgeon

"I love reading I know it's very important and I respect anyone that is patient enough to do it."

— **Stanley Victor Paskavich**

#307

"One of the pleasures of reading is seeing this alteration on the pages, and the way, by reading it, you have made the book yours."

— Paul Theroux

"Books are more precious than jewels. She truly believed this. What did a diamond bring you? A momentary flash of brilliance. A diamond scintillated for second; a book could scintillate forever."

— **Veronica Henry**

#309

"Men of power have not time to read, yet men who do not read are not fit for power. "

— Michael Foot

"Good books are for consideration after, too."

— **Stephen King**

"I just got out of the hospital. I was in a speed-reading accident. I hit a bookmark. "

— Steve Wright

"The man who never reads will never be read; he who never quotes will never be quoted. He who will not use the thoughts of other men's brains, proves that he has no brains of his own. You need to read."

— **Charles Spurgeon**

#313

"There are two kinds of books in the world--the boring kind they make you read in school and the interesting kind that they won't let you read in school because then they would have to talk about real stuff like sex and divorce and is there a God and if there isn't then what happens when you die, and how come the history books have so many lies in them."

— LouAnne Johnson

#314

"You can't keep living without breathing; don't keep living without reading!"

— Ernest Agyemang Yeboah

#315

"The worth of a book is to be measured by what you can carry away from it."

— James Bryce

"If I had any idea of heaven, it was this: shelves and shelves of books, ten times as many as were upstairs, each with stories or pictures more exciting and beautiful than the next, and two overstuffed chairs big enough for me to sleep in."

— Clay Carmichael

"To enjoy and learn from what you read you must understand the meanings of the words a writer uses. You do yourself a grave disservice if you read around words you don't know, or worse, merely guess at what they mean without bothering to look them up.

For me, reading has always been not only a quest for pleasure and enlightenment but also a word-hunting expedition, a lexical safari."

— **Charles Harrington Elster**

"Individuals who frequently read fiction seem to be better able to understand other people, empathize with them and see the world from their perspective."

— **Annie Murphy Paul**

"Read things you're sure will disagree with your current thinking."

— **Joel Salatin**

"We profit little by books we do not enjoy."

— John Lubbock

"Keep on reading, thinking, doing and writing! Words keep introducing their friends to you."

— **Toba Beta**

"The way a book is read- which is to say, the qualities a reader brings to a book- can have as much to do with its worth as anything the author puts into it."

— **Norman Cousins**

#323

"Without a doubt,
I must read,
all the books
I've read about.
See the artworks
hung on hooks,
that I have only,
seen in books."

— **Lang Leav**

"A love affair
with knowledge
will never end
in heartbreak."

— **Michael Marino**

#325

"The paradox of reading is that the path toward ourselves passes through books, but that this must remain a passage. It is a traversal of books that a good reader engages in – a reader who knows that every book is the bearer of part of himself and can give him access to it, if only he has the wisdom not to end his journey there."

— **Pierre Bayard**

#**326**

"It doesn't make sense to read something unless you can absorb the information and apply it to your daily life."

— **Jim Kwik**

"If you cannot read all your books...fondle them — peer into them, let them fall open where they will, read from the first sentence that arrests the eye, set them back on the shelves with your own hands, arrange them on your own plan so that you at least know where they are. Let them be your friends; let them, at any rate, be your acquaintances."

— **Winston Churchill**

#**328**

"You can't enjoy art or books in a hurry."

— E.A. Bucchianeri

"I think reading is part of the birthright of the human being"

— LeVar Burton

"There's no book that absolutely everyone loves."

— Carolyn Parkhurst

"Reading is equivalent to another life."

— **Nitin Namdeo**

"The love of books is among the choicest gifts of the gods."

— Sir Arthur Conan Doyle

"Wisdom, ambition, sadness, joy, malice, grief, amazement, all the emotions which blaze within the human soul may be recorded on a page.

Nestled in a sheaf of paper sleeps an infinity beyond the limits of the universe. Just by opening a single page, we may fly into that infinity."

— **Tanigawa Nagaru**

#**334**

"Great readers (are) those who know early that there is never going to be time to read all there is to read, but do their darnedest anyway."

— **Larry McMurtry**

"You are
what you eat
and read."

— **Maya Corrigan**

"No one ever gets through their TBR list. For every book you finish, you'll add five more. That's just the way it works."

— Leisa Rayven

#337

"The number of books completed is a vanity metric. As you know more, you leave more books unfinished. Focus on new concepts with predictive power."

— Naval RaviKant

"In an established love of reading there is a policy of insurance guaranteeing certain happiness till death."

— A. Edward Newton

#339

"It's just God's gift. If you're into self-education, there's nothing like reading. Of course, people do a lot of it have an enormous advantage."

— Charlie Munger

#340

"Read as many investment books as you can get your hands on. I've been able to learn something from almost every book I have read."

— Lee Ainslie

#341

"Open the
book and read
it to renew
your mind."

— **Lailah Gifty Akita**

#**342**

"Books doesn't advertise on TV because it's customers doesn't watch it."

— Shiromani Kant

#343

"I still love the book-ness of books, the smell of books: I am a book fetishist—books to me are the coolest and sexiest and most wonderful things there are."

— **Neil Gaiman**

#344

"Learning to read is one of the most extraordinary gifts you'll ever receive, so open up God's Word and read the most extraordinary book ever written."

— J.E.B. Spredemann

#345

"Owning a book is a third of the goal. The others are actually reading it and applying it."

— **Israel Wayne**

#346

"You have a false understanding of what it means to read. Reading is not just turning printed signs into sounds. Reading is something deeper. True reading means hearing what the book has to say and pondering it— perhaps even having a conversation in your mind with the author. It means learning about the world— the world as it really is, not as you wish it to be."

— J.M. Coetzee

"Recommending a book to someone is the second best thing to buying it for them, which is the second best thing to reading it for them."

— **Mokokoma Mokhonoana**

#348

"Read today so you
don't bleed tomorrow.
An uninformed human
is a wounded human."

— **Mmanti Umoh**

#349

"Our books can know and remember for us, but cannot think for us."

— **Mokokoma Mokhonoana**

#350

"Knowing too much is the curse of reading."

— Shiromani Kant

#351

"If you ever get bored, let the words scream in your head."

— **Karl Kristian Flores**

"Read books through the lens of life preparation."

— Kelly Gallagher

"Reading together is an activity least talked about, but once you flip pages together, you flip many moments together."

— Akansh Malik

#354

"However vast any person's basic reading may be, there still remain an enormous number of fundamental works that he has not read."

— **Italo Calvino**

"Even people who can't read are impressed by books."

— Octavia E. Butler

#356

"Reading is an act of meeting people that will change your life."

— Shiromani Kant

#357

"Beneath the nice book cover, camera angles, format of the page, size of the canvas, sound of the song – was someone with something to say."

— **Karl Kristian Flores**

"Some haven't read the Bible and yet hate it. To anyone, I say: there is one book on your planet that may have an answer, that has survived ages and debates, and you have never cared to read it? What was so important?"

— **Karl Kristian Flores**

#359

"I am saying that
you should read
everyone else's
story with the
same respect as
you do your own."

— **Syed M. Masood**

"Reading authentic books becomes flowers of knowledge. Experience and vision become a fragrance of knowledge.
To discover and understand that, it is insight."

— **Ehsan Sehgal**

"Reading it in a book does not make it a fact."

— Loren Weisman

"A few books, well studied, and thoroughly digested, nourish the understanding more than hundreds but gargled in the mouth, as ordinary students use."

— **Frances Osborne**

#363

"There is no problem that a library card can't solve."

— **Eleanor Brown**

#364

"The only way to educate oneself is by making books a life companion."

— **Michael Bassey Johnson**

#365

"Books train your mind to imagination to think big."

— **Taylor Swift**

"There is no friend as loyal as a book."

– Ernest Hemingway

#367

"We read to get lost, to forget the hard times we're living in and we read to remember those who came before us who lived through something harder,"

— Jacqueline Woodson

#368

"Your (personal) library is the representation of your strengths."

— Shiromani Kant

"Every man who knows how to read has it in his power to magnify himself, to multiply the ways in which he exists, to make his life full, significant, and interesting."

— **Aldous Huxley**

"We don't need a list of rights and wrongs, tables of dos and don'ts: we need books, time, and silence. Thou shalt not is soon forgotten, but Once upon a time lasts forever."

— **Philip Pullman**

"Reading is everything. Reading makes me feel like I've accomplished something, learned something, become a better person. Reading makes me smarter. Reading gives me something to talk about later on. Reading is the unbelievably healthy way my attention deficit disorder medicates itself. Reading is escape, and the opposite of escape; it's a way to make contact with reality after a day of making things up, and it's a way of making contact with someone else's imagination after a day that's all too real. Reading is grist. Reading is bliss."

— **Nora Ephron**

#372

"Book collecting is an obsession, an occupation, a disease, an addiction, a fascination, an absurdity, a fate. It is not a hobby. Those who do it must do it."

— Jeanette Winterson

#373

"A book is where years of experience and millions of ideas meet."

— Shiromani Kant

#374

"WORDS change WORLDS."

— Pam Allyn

"Proper reading and implimenting secures good fortune."

— Shiromani Kant

#376

"We are oversupplied with people and books that make us know more, but are undersupplied with those that make us think and live better."

— **Mokokoma Mokhonoana**

"Some men think more than they read. Others read more than they think. Those who practice both, grow wise. Those who follow neither, remain ignorant."

— John Leland

#378

"Ever since I discovered how reading stimulates the mind's imagination, I have never stopped reading"

— **James Hauenstein**

"Reading books is good.

Reading and implimenting is better.

Reading, implimenting and sharing is best."

— Shiromani Kant

"If you find it interesting enough to write, someone will find it interesting enough to read."

— **Carmela Dutra**

#381

"A first reading is something special, like first love."

— Graham Greene

#382

"With books, you're never lonely. Your friends are the best minds who have ever lived."

— A.D. Aliwat

"Read widely
because almost
nothing has been
everywhere applied."

— Jesse Ball

#384

"We're all what we read to a very considerable degree."

— David McCullough

#385

"Reading makes a full man, meditation a profound man, discourse a clear man."

— Benjamin Franklin

#386

"A book is but a stack of paper until someone reads it. And when someone reads it, they build a house within its pages so whenever they return to that book, they feel right at home."

— **Caroline George**

#387

"Libraries will get you through times of no money better than money will get you through times of no libraries."

— Anne Herbert

#388

"Let your curiosity be the guide to your reading list."

— Shiromani Kant

#389

"There is no limit to what you can read."

— **Lailah Gifty Akita**

"Take a deep breath and read. It'll calm you."

— Robert Dunbar

"Developed mindset is the by-product of 1000s hours spent reading."

— Shiromani Kant

"A good book leaves you better than the way it found you."

— Craig D. Lounsbrough

#393

"In the morning, nurture your mind with good books. At night, write yours."

— **Michael Bassey Johnson**

#394

"Read the book based on problem you are facing!"

— Akhilesh Bhagwat

"The great
success tool is
reading more
to obtain the
skills you need
to start working
on your dream"

— **Anath Lee Wales**

#**396**

"A book should be an axe to break the frozen sea inside you."

— Ali Smith

#397

"Reading allows us to traverse time, space, one's own consciousness. It engages the mind like nothing else, stimulating every part of the brain and allowing the reader to experience everything as if they were truly there."

— A.D. Aliwat

"A reader has always multiple views for a thing or situation, and this is the blessing of reading."

— Nitin Namdeo

#399

"The personal library is...the archive of a reading life. Or perhaps a mausoleum in which, though sealed away, one lives like nowhere else."

— **Burkhard Spinnen**

"A good book can cure heartbreak."

— Jiu Er,

"Read. Dream. Repeat."

— Richelle E. Goodrich

"There comes a point in your life when you need to stop reading other people's books **and write your own."**

— Albert Einstein

"Reading one page of a book and implementing is much better than reading the book to completion and doing nothing.

Books are meant to be used."

— Mac Duke

"You respect books by using them, not leaving them alone."

— Umberto Eco

"Books are wishing stars fallen to Earth, waiting for people to live their dreams through reading."

— **Richelle E. Goodrich**

"Reading is about enjoying yourself and learning about the human experience, so go for it."

— Jonathan Mooney

"Some books are to be tasted, others to be swallowed, and some few to be chewed and digested; that is, some books are to be read only in parts; others to be read, but not curiously; and some few to be read wholly, and with diligence and attention."

— Francis Bacon

#408

"Read a lot of books. History is shaped by those who read."

— Abdul Malik Omar

"Books have a way of finding their way into our lives, usually, right when we need them the most."

— Richard Cardenas

"Fools read fast. Geniuses reread."

— Maxime Lagacé

"Of all things I liked books the best."

— **Nikola Tesla**

"Reading really is one of the best remedies for stupidity."

— Jon Etter

#413

"If you haven't read hundreds of books, you're functionally illiterate."

— James Mattis

#414

"Books don't have bulbs in them,
But the light they give out, brightens up even the darkest souls!"

— **Azhar Ali Shar**

"Read fiction to open your mind to greater possibilities and read non-fiction to learn the constraints of dreams and the facts that might guide you to attain one."

— Carmine Savastano

"Mind your discipline to read, read to discipline your mind."

— **Mark Hanson**

"If there's a book you really want to read, but it hasn't been written yet, then you must write it."

— Toni Morrison

"I read my books with diligence, and mounting skill, and gathering certainty. I read the way a person might swim, to save his or her life."

— **Mary Oliver**

#**419**

"My job description is reading, which I love to do. We don't have too many meetings and things like that. A good amount of reading is not directly investment-related."

— Mohnish Pabrai

#420

"Reading is perhaps the greatest pleasure you will have in life; the one you will think of longest, and repent of least."

— **William Hazlitt**

"The person, be it gentleman or lady, who has not pleasure in a good novel, must be intolerably stupid."

— Jane Austen

"Becoming a reader is a change for the better. Trust me. No one has ever lost by becoming addicted to stories – to the lessons learned by those who possess enough courage to put pen to paper."

— Ellery Adams

#423

"A person who does not read and never seeks to increase personal knowledge will always remain imprisoned by ignorance and unable to escape a cellblock of drudgery and despair."

— Kilroy J. Oldster

#424

"I absolutely look at people's bookshelves. And I have some judgment. I mean, they're openly showing you themselves."

— **Andrew Sean Greer**

#425

"Reading a book is like exploring the places you can't visit, experiencing the situation you can't experience."

— Nitin Namdeo

"Choosing to buy a particular book over others only or mainly because it is the cheapest is excusable only if you are learning to read."

— **Mokokoma Mokhonoana**

#427

"You can get lost in any library, no matter the size. But the more lost you are, the more things you'll find."

— **Millie Florence**

"Writing and reading decrease our sense of isolation. They deepen and widen and expand our sense of life: they feed the soul"

— Anne Lamott

#429

"After reading a good book, something must change in you! If nothing changed, then you can be sure that you haven't read the book with your soul!"

— Mehmet Murat ildan

"Reading is at the threshold of our inner life; it can lead us into that life but cannot constitute it."

— **Marcel Proust**

"A man only learns by two things; one is reading and the other is association with smarter people."

— Will Rogers

"It's really not about reading a good book. Rather, it about being transformed by great ideas."

— Craig D. Lounsbrough

#433

"Many a book is like a key to unknown chambers within the castle of one's own self."

— Franz Kafka

#434

"A library is not a luxury but one of the necessities of life."

— Henry Ward Beecher

"A book is read one page at a time. A shelf is read one book at a time. A library is read one shelf at a time."

— **Terry Goodkind**

"A good book delivers a great message. And while such a message should touch the reader in a good way, it must transform them in a great way."

— Craig D. Lounsbrough

"Readers are lucky – they will never be bored or lonely."

— Natalie Babbitt

#438

"Either write something worth reading or do something worth writing."

— Benjamin Franklin

#439

"My Alma mater was books, a good library... I could spend the rest of my life reading, just satisfying my curiosity."

— Malcolm X

#440

"The book to read is not the one which thinks for you, but the one which makes you think."

— James McCosh

"Read, every day, something no one else is reading. Think, every day, something no one else is thinking. Do, every day, something no one else would be silly enough to do. It is bad for the mind to continually be part of unanimity."

— **Christopher Morley**

#**442**

"Read in order to live."

— Gustave Flaubert

#443

"A man is known by the books he reads."

— Ralph Waldo Emerson

"Books were my pass to personal freedom. I learned to read at age three, and soon discovered there was a whole world to conquer that went beyond our farm in Mississippi."

— **Oprah Winfrey**

#445

"The only important thing in a book is the meaning that it has for you."

— W. Somerset Maugham

"I can't imagine a man really enjoying a book and reading it only once."

— C. S. Lewis

#447

"When I get a little money I buy books; and if any is left I buy food and clothes."

— **Desiderius Erasmus**

"I divide all readers into two classes: those who read to remember and those who read to forget."

— William Lyon Phelps

#449

"Reading should not be presented to children as a chore or duty. It should be offered to them as a precious gift."

— Kate DiCamillo

#450

"The habit of reading is the only one I know in which there is no alloy. It lasts when all other pleasures fade."

— Anthony Trollope

"Let books be your dining table, **And you shall be full of delights.** *Let them be your mattress,* **And you shall sleep restful nights"**

— **Ephrem the Syrian**

#452

"Books are
the treasured
wealth of the
world and the
fit inheritance
of generations
and nations."

— Henry David Thoreau

#453

"There are three kinds of men. The one that learns by reading. The few who learn by observation. The rest of them have to pee on the electric fence for themselves."

— **Will Rogers**

#454

"We shouldn't teach great books; **we should teach a love of reading.**"

— B. F. Skinner

#455

"Books shouldn't be daunting, they should be funny, exciting and wonderful; and learning to be a reader gives a terrific advantage."

— **Roald Dahl**

#**456**

"A good book is the precious lifeblood of a master spirit."

— John Milton

"God be thanked for books; they are the voices of the distant and the dead, and make us heirs of the spiritual life of past ages."

— **William Ellery Channing**

#458

"You can find magic wherever you look. Sit back and relax, all you need is a book."

— Dr. Seuss

#459

"There are three classes of readers; some enjoy without judgment; others judge without enjoyment; and some there are who judge while they enjoy, and enjoy while they judge. The latter class reproduces the work of art on which it is engaged. Its numbers are very small."

— Johann Wolfgang von Goethe

#460

"If we encounter a man of rare intellect, we should ask him what books he reads."

— Ralph Waldo Emerson

#461

"A book is a garden, an orchard, a storehouse, a party, a company by the way, a counselor, a multitude of counselors."

— **Charles Baudelaire**

#462

"There is a great deal of difference between an eager man who wants to read a book and the tired man who wants a book to read."

— Gilbert K. Chesterton

#463

"Resolve to edge in a little reading every day, if it is but a single sentence. If you gain fifteen minutes a day, it will make itself felt at the end of the year."

— Horace Mann

#464

"A library is the delivery room for the birth of ideas, a place where history comes to life."

— **Norman Cousins**

#465

"What is wonderful about great literature is that it transforms the man who reads it towards the condition of the man who wrote."

— E. M. Forster

#466

"I am a part of everything that I have read."

— Theodore Roosevelt

#467

"I know every book of mine by its smell, and I have but to put my nose between the pages to be reminded of all sorts of things."

— George Gissing

#468

"When you are growing up there are two institutional places that affect you most powerfully: the church, which belongs to God, and the public library, which belongs to you."

— Keith Richards

#469

"Elegance isn't
solely defined by
what you wear.
It's how you
carry yourself,
how you speak,
what you read."

— **Carolina Herrera**

"Perhaps no place in any community is so totally democratic as the town library. The only entrance requirement is interest."

— **Lady Bird Johnson**

#**471**

"We must form our minds by reading deep rather than wide."

— **Quintilian**

"Always read something that will make you look good if you die in the middle of it."

— P. J. O'Rourke

#473

"It is not enough to simply teach children to read; we have to give them something worth reading."

— Katherine Paterson

"The world of books is the most remarkable creation of man."

— Clarence Day

"All good books are alike in that they are truer than if they really happened and after you are finished reading one you feel that it all happened to you and after which it all belongs to you."

— **Ernest Hemingway**

#**476**

"Education begins the gentleman, but reading, good company, and reflection must finish him."

— John Locke

"The best effect of any book is that it excites the reader to self activity."

— **Thomas Carlyle**

#**478**

"Choose an author as you choose a friend."

— Christopher Wren

#479

"Books are like mirrors: if a fool looks in, you cannot expect a genius to look out."

— J. K. Rowling

"One can transform a place by reading in it."

— Alberto Manguel

#481

"Don't ask me who's influenced me. A lion is made up of the lambs he's digested, and I've been reading all my life."

— **Charles de Gaulle**

#482

"I have a real soft spot in my heart for librarians and people who care about books."

— **Ann Richards**

#483

"Some women have a weakness for shoes... I can go barefoot if necessary. I have a weakness for books."

— **Oprah Winfrey**

"The writer who breeds more words than he needs, is making a chore for the reader who reads."

— Dr. Seuss

#485

"When I discovered libraries, it was like having Christmas every day."

— Jean Fritz

#486

"All the glory of the world would be buried in oblivion, unless God had provided mortals with the remedy of books."

— **Richard de Bury**

#487

"Read books are far less valuable than unread ones. The library should contain as much of what you do not know as your financial means, mortgage rates, and the currently tight real-estate market alow you to put there."

— **Nassim Nicholas Taleb**

#488

"Reading a book is like re-writing it for yourself. You bring to a novel, anything you read, all your experience of the world. You bring your history and you read it in your own terms."

— Angela Carter

#489

"Nothing is worth reading that does not require an alert mind."

— **Charles Dudley Warner**

#490

"Pity the man who has a favorite restaurant, but not a favorite author. He's picked out a favorite place to feed his body, but he doesn't have a favorite place to feed his mind!"

— Jim Rohn

#491

"I read hard, or not at all; never skimming, never turning aside to merely inciting books; and Plato, Aristotle, Butler, Thucydides, Sterne, Jonathan Edwards, have passed like the iron atoms of the blood into my mental constitution."

— Frederick William Robertson

#492

"To feel most beautifully alive means to be reading something beautiful."

— Gaston Bachelard

#493

"Force yourself to reflect on what you read, paragraph by paragraph."

— Samuel Taylor Coleridge

"Learn to read slow; all other graces will follow in their proper places."

— **William Walker**

"Reading is seeing by proxy."

— **Herbert Spencer**

"A book is the only place in which you can examine a fragile thought without breaking it."

— Charles Scribner IV

#497

"Anyone who reads a book with a sense of obligation does not understand the art of reading."

— Lin Yutang

"Reading is a means of thinking with another person's mind; it forces you to stretch your own."

— **Charles Scribner IV**

#499

"That is a good book which is opened with expectation, and closed with delight and profit."

— Amos Bronson Alcott

"In a library we are surrounded by many hundreds of dear friends, but they are imprisoned by an enchanter in these paper and leathern boxes."

— **Ralph Waldo Emerson**

"Until I feared
I would lose it,
I never loved
to read. One
does not love
breathing."

— Harper Lee

"Remember, young man, experience is not the best teacher. Other people's experience is the best teacher. By reading about the lives of great people, you can unlock the secrets to what made them great."

— Andy Andrews

#**503**

"The Only way to do all the things you'd like to do is to read."

— **Tom Clancy**

"He has only half learned the art of reading who has not added to it the more refined art of skipping and skimming."

— Arthur Balfour

#505

"The unread story is not a story; it is little black marks on wood pulp. The reader, reading it, makes it live: a live thing, a story."

— **Ursula K. Le Guin**

#506

"The books that help you most are those which make you think that most. The hardest way of learning is that of easy reading; but a great book that comes from a great thinker is a ship of thought, deep freighted with truth and beauty."

— **Pablo Neruda**

#507

"The worst thing about new books is that they keep us from reading the old ones."

— **Joseph Joubert**

"Of all the diversions of life, there is none so proper to fill up its empty spaces as the reading of useful and entertaining authors."

— **Joseph Addison**

#509

"One always tends to overpraise a long book, because one has got through it."

— E. M. Forster

"Reading is not a duty, and has consequently no business to be made disagreeable."

— **Aneurin Bevan**

"We are now in want of an art to teach how books are to be read rather than to read them. Such an art is practicable."

— **Benjamin Disraeli**

"Learn to be good readers, which is perhaps a more difficult thing than you imagine. Learn to be discriminative in your reading; to read faithfully, and with your best attention, all kinds of things which you have a real interest in,--a real, not an imaginary,--and which you find to be really fit for what you are engaged in."

— **Thomas Carlyle**

#513

"It is not the reading of many books which is necessary to make a man wise or good, but the well-reading of a few, could he be sure to have the best. And it is not possible to read over many on the same subject without a great deal of loss of precious time."

— Richard Baxter

#514

"People seldom read a book which is given to them; and few are given. The way to spread a work is to sell it at a low price. No man will send to buy a thing that costs even sixpence without an intention to read it."

— Samuel Johnson

"**Read as much as you can, discarding negative or disturbing information. Learn by doing, and the Goddess and God will bless you with all that you truly need.**"

— Scott Cunningham

#**516**

"We need to tell kids flat out: *reading is not optional.*"

— Walter Dean Myers

"Reading is the gateway skill that makes all other learning possible."

— Barack Obama

"Digital reading will completely take over. It's lightweight and it's fantastic for sharing. Over time it will take over."

— **Bill Gates**

#519

"Keep reading books, but remember that a book's only a book, and you should learn to think for yourself."

— **Maxim Gorky**

"Love of books is the best of all."

— Jackie Kennedy

"We should always choose our books as God chooses our friends, just a bit beyond us, so that we have to do our level best to keep up with them."

— **Oswald Chambers**

"Literacy is much more than an educational priority - it is the ultimate investment in the future and the first step towards all the new forms of literacy required in the twenty-first century. We wish to see a century where every child is able to read and to use this skill to gain autonomy."

— Irina Bokova

"Text is just ink
on a page until
a reader comes
along and gives
it life."

— Louise Rosenblatt

"Fairy tales are more than true: not because they tell us that dragons exist, but because they tell us that dragons can be beaten."

— Neil Gaiman

#525

"The genuine love for reading itself, when cultivated, is a superpower."

— Naval RaviKant

#526

"Some people claim that it is okay to read trashy novels because sometimes you can find something valuable in them. You can also find a crust of bread in a garbage can, if you search long enough, *but* there is a better way."

— **Jim Rohn**

#527

"Books are written by the alone for the alone."

— Donna Tartt

"Reading a book isn't a race — the better the book, the more slowly it should be read."

— Naval RaviKant

"The man who has not the habit of reading is imprisoned in his immediate world."

— Lin Yutang

"You can make positive deposits in your own economy every day by reading and listening to powerful, positive, life-changing content and by associating with encouraging and hope-building people."

— Zig Ziglar

#531

"Reading is the occupation of the insomniac par excellence."

— Alberto Manguel

"If you are going to get anywhere in life you have to read a lot of books."

— **Roald Dahl**

"We read to understand, or to begin to understand."

— **Alberto Manguel**

"It is impossible to enslave, mentally or socially, a bible-reading people. The principles of the bible are the groundwork of human freedom."

— **Horace Greeley**

"It almost doesn't matter what you read. Eventually, you will read enough things (and your interests will lead you there) that will dramatically improve your life."

— Naval RaviKant

#**536**

"Whether it is fun to go to bed with a good book depends a great deal on who's reading it."

— Bill Vaughan

#537

"Books are to be called for and supplied on the assumption that the process of reading is not a half-sleep, but in the highest sense an exercise, a gymnastic struggle; that the reader is to do something for himself."

— **Walt Whitman**

"Reading... changes you."

— Margaret Atwood

"If reading becomes a bore, mental death is on the way."

— Joan Aiken

"Students need to make their own choices about reading material and writing topics."

— Donalyn Miller

#541

"No ornament of a house can compare with books; they are constant company in a room, even when you are not reading them."

— Harriet Beecher Stowe

#**542**

"Reading
becomes the fuel
for development."

— Narendra Modi

#543

"Reading a book should be a conversation between you and the author. Presumably he knows more about the subject than you do; if not, you probably should not be bothering with his book."

— **Mortimer Adler**

"Reading is the subtle and thorough sharing of the ideas and feelings by underhanded means. It is a gross invasion of Privacy and a direct violation of the Constitutions of the Third, Fourth, and Fifth Age. The Teaching of Reading is equally a crime against Privacy and Personhood. One to five years on each count."

— **Walter Tevis**

#545

"Reading is one of the most individual things that happens. So every reader is going to read a piece in a slightly different way, sometimes a radically different way."

— Margaret Atwood

#546

"Reading wasn't my religion - it was my oxygen."

— Linda Grant

"If a book has no index or good table of contents, it is very useful to make one as you are reading it."

— Isaac

"I spend the bulk of
my day reading
the work of others
whom I respect."

— **Frank Martin**

#549

"Never stop reading. History doesn't repeat but it does rhyme."

— **Seth Klarman**

"**The more and more and more we read, the more interconnected the world becomes, the more we recognize patterns, the more we are able to 'follow the threads."**

— Christopher Begg

"You should be a
voracious reader and a
sponge of information
from other investors.
With all the ideas out
there, you do not have
to agree with them or
adopt them, but you
should consider them."

— **Larry Robbins**

#552

"I have learned more from reading than from formal education."

— Roy Neuberger

#553

"At some point you have to stop reading, and start doing."

— **Ruchika Tomar**

"Enough reading, time for action."

— A.D. Aliwat

For more content from books and about books,

Follow me on my social media handles:

instagram.com/readerpreneur
twitter.com/readerpreneur

Made in United States
Orlando, FL
10 May 2022

17735694R00338